**by Paul Ladewski**

# SCHOLASTIC INC.

New York   Toronto   London   Auckland   Sydney

Mexico City   New Delhi   Hong Kong   Buenos Aires

Special thanks to Bree Stewart for her help on this project.
— P.L.

**PHOTO CREDITS**
All photos are © NBA/Getty Images
Front cover: Doug Benc
Noah Graham (4, 15, 16); Ronald Martinez (6); Jennifer Pottheiser (7);
Jamie Squire (8); Nathaniel S. Butler (9, 22); Fernando Medina (11);
Andrew D. Bernstein (13, 14); Paul Buck (17); Jesse D. Garrabrant (18, 19);
Gregory Shamus (20, 31); Stephen Dunn (21); Glenn James (23, 26);
David Sherman (25, 27); Eliot J. Schechter (29)

ISBN-13: 978-0-439-91239-6
ISBN-10: 0-439-91239-3

12  11  10  9  8  7  6  5  4  3  2  1        7  8  9  10  11/0

Printed in the U.S.A.
First printing, February 2007
Book design: Kim Brown, Cheung Tai, and Henry Ng

# Contents

# *Introduction*

The top guards in the NBA come in different shapes and sizes. They also come from different backgrounds and even different countries. At the same time, they all have one important thing in common: the determination to be the best no matter what obstacles are in the way.

Many experts said that there was no room for Gilbert Arenas in the NBA, but he never lost faith in his ability.

Chauncey Billups bounced from team to team before his talents blossomed.

Told he was too small to play a big man's game, Allen Iverson became a star nonetheless.

Steve Nash grew up in hockey-mad Canada, only to develop into one of the greatest basketball players ever produced there.

LeBron James and Dwyane Wade overcame difficult childhoods to become two of the brightest young stars in the league.

And Kobe Bryant and Tracy McGrady took a

different and more difficult route to the top — from high school straight to the professional ranks.

The best players at this position have leadership ability. They can make split-second decisions. They know when to pass the ball to a teammate, shoot it, or take it to the hoop. The better ones also take pride in their defense. But it is their will to succeed that sets them all apart from the rest.

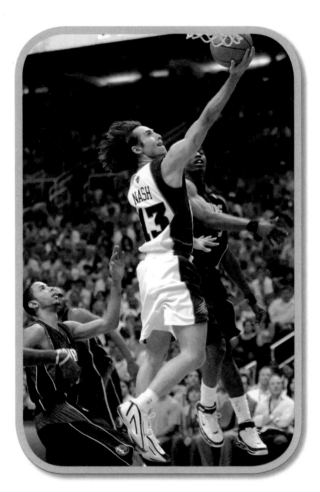

# Gilbert Arenas

*T*hud, thud, thud. *Squeak, squeak, squeak. Swish, swish, swish.* While the world around him sleeps, Washington Wizards guard Gilbert Arenas practices in a dimly lit gym. It is three o'clock in the morning.

Workouts in the wee hours and odd superstitions set Gilbert apart from other players. To Wizards fans, his behavior is known as Gilbertology. For example, how did Gilbert decide which team to sign with from the many who wanted him? He flipped a coin ten times. The Wizards won.

Gilbert practices the same routine before, during, and after every game. He eats the same meal, dresses in the same order, and listens to the same music. After every game, he tosses his jersey to someone in the crowd. Gilbert used to throw his sneakers, too, but now he wears the same ones until the Wizards lose a game. Once, during half-time of a game against the San Antonio Spurs, he took a shower in his full uniform as a way to wash off any bad luck and start over again. Gilbert also likes to pull pranks — it's not unusual for him to hide the jersey of a Wizards teammate before the game.

Mostly, the super-quick Gilbert likes to prove people wrong. That is why he wears the num-

ber zero on his jersey. While Gilbert attended the University of Arizona, doubters said he would play zero minutes if he was drafted by an NBA team. Gilbert played more than that . . . a lot more. In the 2005–2006 season, his 3,384 minutes led the league. Gilbert would probably request 3,384 as his uniform number next season, except that players are only allowed two-digit numbers.

Time and again, Gilbert has had to prove himself. Before the 6 foot 4 greyhound entered the

2001 NBA draft, he was called a "tweener" by many scouts. That meant he was too short to play shooting guard but not a strong enough ball-handler to play point guard. Selected in the second round by the Golden State Warriors, Gilbert sat on the bench at the start of the season.

So Gilbert treated every practice like a game. He watched hours and hours of game tape. He predicted he would be a starter after the All-Star break. Almost nobody believed him except Gilbert himself, but sure enough, he started the last thirty games of the season.

Raised by his father in Hollywood, California, Gilbert became an All-Star in his fourth season in the league. That same 2004–2005 season, he led the Wizards to their first playoff appearance in ten years. The Wizard of Ah's hit a shot at the buzzer to beat the Chicago Bulls and help his team advance to the second round.

Gilbert has made a lot of noise in a short amount of time as an NBA player. If he has his way, we haven't heard the last of it. *Thud, thud, thud. Squeak, squeak, squeak. Swish, swish, swish.*

# Chauncey Billups

Chauncey Billups is known as Mr. Big Shot around the league. The reason is simple—the Detroit Pistons point guard isn't afraid to take and make big shots late in close games. He also has been called Smooth because of the way he plays the game.

But there's a name that fits Chauncey better, one that he likes even more. That name is Winner.

Since Chauncey arrived in 2002, the Pistons have become the first team since the Chicago Bulls in the early 1990s to reach the conference finals in four straight years. They were the league champions in the 2003–2004 season, when Chauncey was named NBA Finals Most Valuable Player. The Pistons nearly won again the next season, losing a heartbreaker against the San Antonio Spurs in the seventh and final game. Had the Pistons hung on to win, Chauncey would likely have been the MVP for the second time in a row.

Things did not always go so smoothly for Smooth, though. Before he was Mr. Big Shot, Chauncey sat on the bench with five different teams in five seasons. In fact he was traded three times before his twenty-fourth birthday! Before Chauncey became the Pistons floor leader, he was concerned he would never find his niche in the league.

The third overall pick in the 1997 NBA draft, Chauncey was dealt from the Boston Celtics to the Toronto Raptors midway through his first season. The one-time University of Colorado star thought he had found the right place in 1998, when he was traded to the Denver Nuggets, his hometown team.

In a game against Sacramento on December 16, 1999, Chauncey and Kings forward Predrag Stojakovic charged for a loose ball. After Stojakovic brought an elbow down hard into his left shoulder, all that Chauncey could remember was shooting pain. It was his final game of the season.

As it turned out, that play was also the beginning of the end for his Nuggets career. In February 2000, Chauncey was sent to Orlando, but he did not play a single minute with the Magic because of the injury. Only three years after his NBA future appeared to be so bright, Chauncey was told he should play in Europe. He calls it the lowest moment of his career.

Then Chauncey received a phone call that changed his life.

Pistons general manager Joe Dumars saw the potential in Chauncey that few others did. Dumars was once a star Pistons guard himself, a key member with two championship teams. It just so happened that Billups grew up a Pistons fan and Dumars was his favorite player.

The match was made in basketball heaven. Like the Pistons, Chauncey is known for his defense and team play. And like the Pistons, who had a 12–3 record when they faced elimination in the last four playoffs, Chauncey is usually at his best when his back is against the wall.

It appears Chauncey Billups has finally found a home.

# Kobe Bryant

I n a game on January 22, 2006, the Toronto Raptors led the Los Angeles Lakers by 63–49 at halftime. At that point, Lakers star guard Kobe Bryant had 26 points, which was an impressive total but nothing that he hadn't done before.

In the second half, however, Kobe would make history.

In the third quarter, Kobe came out on fire and scored 27 points. In the fourth quarter, he totaled 28 more points. Incredibly, Kobe scored 55 points in the second half for a total of 81 points in the game! It was the most points scored by one player since 1962, when a giant named Wilt Chamberlain scored 100 points, a record that still stands today.

The only modern player who even flirted with the record was David Robinson in 1994, when he scored 71 points. Both Robinson and Chamberlain were 7 foot 1 centers who were much taller than the majority of their opponents. When you consider that Kobe is seven inches shorter, his 81-point game is even more impressive.

Then again, very few players have been able to put the ball in the basket like Kobe has in his career. Kobe and Chamberlain are the only players in NBA history to score 35 or more points in thirteen consecutive games. Kobe is also one of only three players to have at least 40 points in nine consecutive games. The other two? Chamberlain and Michael Jordan.

Kobe is one of many players whose style has been compared to that of Jordan over the years. Like the former Chicago Bulls superstar, Kobe is a 6 foot 6 guard. And like Jordan, Kobe can react quicker and jump higher than anyone his size. And only Kobe has come close to Jordan in his accomplishments on the court.

Jordan finished his fifteen-year career with six NBA titles, ten scoring crowns, and a regular-season average of 30.1 points per game, the highest in history. (The most points Jordan totaled in one contest was 69 in 1990). So far, Kobe owns three league championships, one scoring title, and a career average of 23.9 points per game. Kobe is only twenty-seven years old, so he has plenty of time to pad those numbers.

Every year many players enter the NBA draft with high expectations. Only a few reach them. The son of Joe "Jellybean" Bryant, a former NBA player, Kobe is one of the few who has lived up to his potential. If he continues to stay healthy, there should be more history ahead of him.

# Allen Iverson

Listed at 6 feet and 165 pounds, give or take an inch and a few ounces, Allen Iverson is almost always the smallest player on the court. But the Philadelphia 76ers floor leader has always played like he's a foot taller. Because what A.I. lacks in height, he makes up for in talent, smarts, and courage.

Or as Allen likes to put it, "I don't play with my size; I just play with my heart."

Even though Allen was an NBA star almost from the day he entered the league ten years ago, football was his favorite sport in high school. He played every position from quarterback to safety and broke several records.

But his mother, Ann, wanted Allen to play basketball. When her son was a small boy, Ann dragged him to his first basketball practice. Allen cried all the way out the door, but it wasn't long before he was hooked on hoops.

Allen lived in a small house on Jordan Drive, a street with the same name as his favorite basketball player, Michael Jordan. As a kid, he wanted to be like Mike. Little did Allen know that he would actually play against his idol one day.

Named Virginia High School Basketball Player and Football Player of the Year in the same season, Allen was so good at both football and basketball that he could have played either sport in college. He chose basketball and Georgetown University in Washington, D.C., where  he was a star just like in high school. After two years, Allen decided it was time to pursue his dream to be a professional player.

The 76ers selected Allen as the first overall pick of the 1996 NBA draft. A.I. didn't play like a rookie—he scored 40 or more points in a record five consecutive games. Allen also became known for his crossover dribble, a move in which he would take the ball one way, then suddenly change direction at the same speed. While help-less opponents were frozen in their steps, Allen could drive to the hoop for an easy basket.

Allen became known as The Answer around the league because he was the solution to almost any problem on the court. Yet there was one question that Allen couldn't solve by himself: Why didn't the 76ers win more than twenty-two games in his first season? The team decided the answer was a new head coach.

So the 76ers hired Larry Brown, who eventually moved Allen from point guard to shooting guard, where he could take better advantage of his abil-ity to score the ball. Sure enough, Allen excelled at his new posi-tion, even being named the top scorer in the league four times.

Allen can do a lot more with a basketball than just dribble and shoot it. In the 2004–2005 season, he became one of only three players ever to rank among the top five in points, steals, and assists in the league. With a career-high 596 assists, A.I. joined Jordan on the short list of players who averaged at least 30 points and 8 assists per game in one season.

# LeBron James

**A** rare blend of size, strength, youth, and athleticism, Cleveland Cavaliers superstar LeBron James definitely is special on a basketball court.

In his junior year at St. Vincent–St. Mary High School in Akron, Ohio, LeBron was crowned with the nickname King James. Had he entered the NBA draft that spring, LeBron would likely have been the first overall pick. But according to the rules, a player had to be over eighteen years old to be eligible.

By his senior year, King James was already a household name. Almost all future NBA players are the stars of their high school basketball teams, but LeBron was so ahead of his time that his games could be seen on national television. In fact, nearly two million households tuned in to watch the player who already had been called the next Michael Jordan.

Yet life wasn't always easy for the kid who would be King.

When LeBron was born on December 30, 1984, in Akron, his mother, Gloria, was only sixteen years old. His father, Anthony, had just been released from prison. Gloria found it difficult to work and attend school at the same time. She and LeBron didn't always have a place to call home.

But even then, Baby James showed his talent. Before LeBron could utter his first word, he had a basketball in his hands. He would play with a foam mini-ball and miniature hoop for hours at a time. It wasn't long before it became obvious that LeBron wasn't like kids his own age. In high school, he was a man among boys. He was already 6 foot 8, and his body was muscular and toned.

In the 2003 draft, LeBron was the first overall pick. Few if any players ever came into the league under more pressure. LeBron had the body and skills that were necessary to achieve greatness, but he was selected by his hometown Cavaliers, a lackluster team that he was expected to turn into a playoff contender immediately.

The extraordinary part of the King James story is that he is as good, if not better, than everyone expects at this point. In his first season, at only nineteen years of age, LeBron averaged 20.9 points, 5.9 assists, and 5.5 rebounds per game. He was the youngest player to be chosen as NBA Rookie of the Year. He was also the youngest to score 50 points in one game as well as reach the 1,000 through 6,000 point marks in his career.

Yet, for all his indi- vidual accomplish- ments, it was the way that James carried the Cavaliers to the second round of the playoffs last spring that suggests he is ready to take another giant step soon. Already King, LeBron awaits the chance to be crowned a champion one day.

# Tracy McGrady

A kid with dreams of a baseball career, Tracy McGrady grew up in Auburndale, Florida, an hour away from Orlando. His mother, Melanise, worked as a maid at a Disney World hotel. Little did they know that eventually Orlando would be home to another magic kingdom, and Tracy would be the star of its NBA team called the Magic.

Known as Pumpkin Head in his youth, Tracy showed little basketball talent. He didn't even make the varsity team his first two years in high school. But by his junior year, Tracy had developed into a solid player with lots of potential.

Yet, while Tracy was the best player on the court, he was not the best student in the classroom. One day after a confrontation with a teacher, Tracy was kicked off the team. It seemed that he had no chance to play in college. That's when Alvis Smith, his former youth team coach, got Tracy an invitation to a well-known summer basketball camp.

When Tracy arrived there, he was a nobody. But everyone knew Tracy when he left. On the first day of camp, he asked to be matched up against future NBA player Lamar Odom, who was considered to be the best of the group. Not only did Tracy turn in an impressive performance against Odom, but he dunked over the head of another top player. Afterward, almost every college recruiter wanted Tracy to play with his team.

After a sensational senior year at Mount Zion Christian Academy in Durham, North Carolina, however, Tracy wasn't certain that college was for him. Many coaches and scouts told Tracy that he would be a sure first-round selection in the 1997 NBA draft. They were right — the Toronto Raptors selected him as the ninth pick in round one.

His first professional season didn't turn out as well as Tracy would have liked, however. He spent a lot of time on the bench while the Raptors lost seventeen games in a row at one point. Tracy had better luck as time went on, and he even helped the team make its first trip to the playoffs.

It wasn't until Tracy signed with the Magic in 2000 that his career took off. After star teammate Grant Hill went down with an ankle injury, Tracy was asked to carry the load. He never trained harder — he strapped weights to his arms and legs and ran sprints and long distances. With the help of his jump shot, which is one of the best in the league, Tracy scored half of the team's points in some games.

In 2004, the Houston Rockets acquired Tracy in a seven-player trade. With Tracy and Yao Ming, the 7 foot 5 center, the Rockets have one of the best outside-inside combinations in the league. With two league scoring crowns and six NBA All-Star Game appearances to his credit at twenty-seven years of age, Tracy has only an NBA championship left to accomplish.

# Steve Nash

The first thing one might have notice about Steve Nash has nothing to do with basketball. It was his rather long, stringy hair. The Phoenix Suns guard and two-time NBA Most Valuable Player appeared to have just walked out of a shower. Either that or he was the target of a water gun.

Then again, from his roots to his talents, Steve is different from most of the rest.

Born in South Africa, Steve moved to Canada with his family when he was young. Steve wasn't always sure that basketball was for him. In fact, his first sport was one that isn't even played with hands — soccer. He also played lacrosse, hockey, and rugby. Steve didn't pick up a basketball until he was in eighth grade.

Once he started to play basketball, though, Steve couldn't give it up. He was the star of his high school soccer and basketball teams. He was invited to play with the Canadian national soccer team, but that would have taken all of his time. Steve had a difficult decision to make — follow in his father's footsteps and play soccer, or play basketball. Steve followed his heart and played basketball.

His high school coach, Ian Hyde-Lay, believed that Steve could play Division I college basketball in the United States. He sent letters and video clips to more than thirty schools. All of them sent the same response — thanks, but no thanks. For motivation, Steve put the letters in a shoebox, which he keeps to this day.

Only Santa Clara State wanted Steve on its team. In Canada, his friends jokingly called it Santa Claus State, because Santa Clara sounded like Santa Claus. To Santa Clara, Steve was like an early Christmas present. In the first round of the 1993 NCAA Tournament, Steve led the Broncos past Arizona in one of the biggest upsets in tourney history.

Three years and two tournament appearances later, some considered Steve to be one of the most polished players in the 1996 NBA draft. Still, some scouts had doubts because of his lack of size and athleticism.

It took a few years, but Steve eventually proved he belonged in the NBA and he proved it in a big way. In 2000, two years after he was traded from the Suns to the Dallas Mavericks, Steve enjoyed a breakout season. He averaged 15.61 points and 7.3 assists per game and was named NBA Comeback Player of the Year.

In 2004, after six seasons with the Mavericks, Steve returned to the Suns as a free agent. There he became the leader of a small, athletic team that played a run-and-gun style, which was an ideal fit for his abilities as a passer and ball-handler. It wasn't long before the Suns became one of the most exciting teams in the league. Better yet, they won thirty-three more games than the previous season, a main reason why Steve was selected MVP for the first time.

Even with injured star Amaré Stoudemire out of action, the Suns continued to shine last season. With Steve in a lead role once again, they advanced to the Western Conference finals. Now Steve has two MVP awards, which he can use as bookends for the shoebox filled with rejection letters.

# Dwyane Wade

There were smiley faces galore in the Miami Heat locker room shortly after they captured the NBA championship on a late night in Dallas last June. But it was the twenty-four-year-old guard with the tilted hat and the shy smile, named Dwyane Wade, for whom everybody seemed to be most happy. Not that Jack Fitzgerald was surprised any.

Fitzgerald coached Dwyane at Richards High School in Oak Lawn, Illinois, not far from where the future star was born. Dwyane was the most talented athlete on the team, but what set him apart even more was his humble attitude and likeable personality.

"It's unusual for the best player on a high school team to also be the most popular one, but his teammates considered Dwyane to be cool, a person they could trust," Fitzgerald recalls. "He wasn't

one to take credit for any success we had as a team. We all know how good Dwyane is on the court, but what makes me most proud is the way he handles himself off it."

For the guy known as D-Wade and Flash, the road from the hard, cold streets of south Chicago to the warm, sunny beaches of Miami had its share of bumps along the way.

When Dwyane was a young child, his parents went their separate ways. Because his mother was poor, Dwyane and his older sister, Tragil, didn't have a real home. When Dwyane was eight years old, Tragil decided to take him away from the drugs, gangs, and violence that he saw each day.

Only thirteen herself, Tragil wanted her younger brother to have a male role model in his life. So the two hopped aboard a bus — Tragil told Dwyane that they were headed to the movies — and they went to their father's home.

The trip would change Dwyane forever, because he discovered a passion for basketball a short time later. In addition to his stepbrothers, Dwyane played with a girl named Siohvaughn Funches, who would eventually become his wife.

Dwyane Sr. coached his son every day. He made sure Junior played basketball the right way. He also preached the benefits of a never-say-die attitude. This proved to be an important lesson for

Dwyane in his sophomore year, when he failed to make the high school varsity team.

As Dwyane saw his game grow, so did his body by as much as three inches in one summer. In 2002, near the end of his sophomore year at Marquette University, some scouts predicted he would become an NBA star. One year later, the Heat selected him as the fifth pick in the draft.

In only three seasons since then, Dwyane has rapidly developed into one of the most electric players in basketball. Last season he led the Heat to their first trip to the NBA Finals. Not only did he average 34.7 points per game, but he became the third youngest player to be selected Most Valuable Player of the series.

To hear Flash tell it, we haven't seen the last of him or his team. "When you have one title, you get greedy," he says. "Now we want two."